RABBIT-PROOF FENCE

The Aborigines were the first people in Australia. They were living there long before the white man came south from Europe, bringing his animals, his illnesses, his way of living, his ideas, his government . . . and his laws.

One law in the early 1900s was about mixed-race children, or 'half-castes' as they were called at that time. This law said that these children – of Aboriginal mothers and white fathers – should be taken away from their families and sent to government or church settlements, to be trained to become servants and farm workers. The Australian government believed it would be better for these children to learn the white man's ways, to learn to behave and think like 'Europeans'.

This is the true story of Molly, Daisy, and Gracie, children aged fourteen, eight, and ten, who were taken away from their families and sent to the Moore River Settlement. But they escaped and walked home, 1600 kilometres across Western Australia.

Seventy years later Doris, Molly's daughter, listened to her mother and her aunty Daisy talking, and realized that this was a story that the world should hear – the story of a famous escape, of a long long walk . . . a story of cold and hunger, heartache and fear . . . a story of great courage and determination . . .

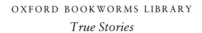

OXFORD BOOKWORMS LIBRARY

True Stories

Rabbit-Proof Fence

Stage 3 (1000 headwords)

Series Editor: Jennifer Bassett
Founder Editor: Tricia Hedge
Activities Editors: Jennifer Bassett and Christine Lindop

*"We followed that fence, the rabbit-proof fence,
all the way home from the settlement to Jigalong.
Long way, alright. We stay in the bush
hiding there for a long time."*

Molly Kelly (born Molly Craig), aged about 79

*To all of my mother's and aunty's children
and their descendants
for inspiration, encouragement and determination.*

Doris Pilkington Garimara,
daughter of Molly Kelly

DORIS PILKINGTON GARIMARA

Rabbit-Proof Fence

Retold by
Jennifer Bassett

OXFORD UNIVERSITY PRESS

OXFORD
UNIVERSITY PRESS

Great Clarendon Street, Oxford OX2 6DP

Oxford University Press is a department of the University of Oxford.
It furthers the University's objective of excellence in research, scholarship,
and education by publishing worldwide in

Oxford New York

Auckland Cape Town Dar es Salaam Hong Kong Karachi
Kuala Lumpur Madrid Melbourne Mexico City Nairobi
New Delhi Shanghai Taipei Toronto

With offices in

Argentina Austria Brazil Chile Czech Republic France Greece
Guatemala Hungary Italy Japan Poland Portugal Singapore
South Korea Switzerland Thailand Turkey Ukraine Vietnam

Original edition copyright © Doris Pilkington Garimara
First published in Australia by University of Queensland Press

This simplified edition © Oxford University Press 2008
Oxford University Press (maker)
First published in Oxford Bookworms 2006

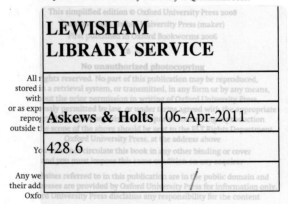

LEWISHAM
LIBRARY SERVICE

No unauthorized photocopying

Askews & Holts	06-Apr-2011
428.6	

ISBN 978 0 19 479144 1

Printed in China

ACKNOWLEDGEMENTS

Photographs are from the motion picture *Rabbit-Proof Fence* and are provided and
reproduced courtesy of the Australian Film Finance Corporation, the Premium Movie
Partnership, South Australian Film Corporation and Jabal Films Pty Limited

Map by Gareth Riddiford

Word count (main text): 10,600 words

For more information on the Oxford Bookworms Library,
visit www.oup.com/bookworms

CONTENTS

NOTE ON THE LANGUAGE

There are many varieties of English spoken in the world, and the people in this story speak a variety of Australian English that sometimes uses non-standard forms (for example, *gunna* for *going to*, and leaving out auxiliary verbs such as *are* and *is*). This is how Doris Pilkington Garimara, the author of the original book, represented the spoken language that her mother and her aunties actually used.

THE FENCE

IT WAS 1,834 kilometres long, and ran from the Southern Ocean near Esperance in the south, to Eighty Mile Beach north of Port Hedland on the north coast.

It was built in 1907, to keep the rabbits out of Western Australia. When the white man first arrived in the country, he brought strange new animals with him – horses, cows, sheep . . . and rabbits. Before long there were thousands and thousands of rabbits, eating all the grass meant for the cows and the sheep. The government of the time believed that a good, strong fence would stop the rabbits moving west into farmlands. The plan did not work, of course, because there were already more rabbits on the Western Australian side of the fence than there were on the South Australian side.

But the rabbit-proof fence became an important landmark for everyone. And when the Mardudjara people – the Mardu – began to move out of the Western Desert, they used to follow the fence to the government depot at Jigalong.

1

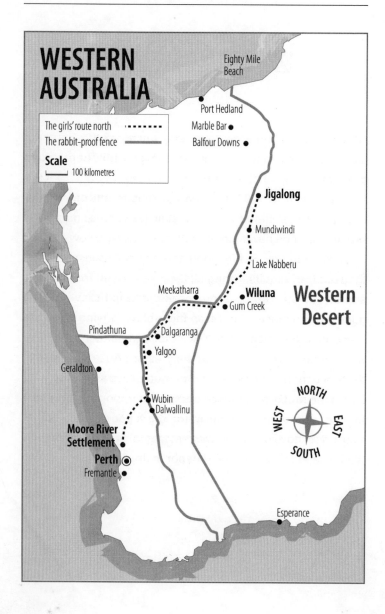

1
Growing up at Jigalong

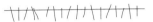

JIGALONG WAS A long way from anywhere, right out in the desert. In the early years it was just a small depot for the white men who worked on the rabbit-proof fence. They rode on horses up and down the fence, clearing away branches of trees and dead animals, and mending holes made by fire or storms or kangaroos.

There was also a government store at Jigalong, which gave out free food, clothing, and blankets to the local people. And in the 1930s the Mardu people decided that Jigalong would be a good place for them to stay. It became a new home, a 'sitting down place' for their people.

Molly grew up at Jigalong, among her people, the Mardu. Her mother, Maude, was a young Mardu woman who used to work as a domestic servant for the superintendent at the depot. Her father was Thomas Craig, an Englishman who worked as an inspector of the rabbit-proof fence. He called the baby Molly, after his sister, and often brought her presents of clothing and dresses. But after a few years his work on the fence finished, and he moved on.

Molly was a pretty child, but while she was still quite young, she already knew she was different, because her skin colour was not as dark as the other Mardu children's.

'You not Mardu, you not wudgebulla!' the children used to shout at her. 'You nothing! You just a mongrel dog!'

Molly used to throw stones at them, or chase them with a stick, but the words still hurt her. So she was very pleased one day when her mother said:

'I got some news for you. Two of your aunties have had babies, little girls, and they're both muda-mudas, like you.'

'They coming to Jigalong?' asked Molly, very excited.

'Yes, very soon,' said Maude.

'What are their names?' Molly asked.

'Gracie and Daisy. They're both younger than you, but they'll be nice friends for you.'

Molly was very happy. 'I got two sisters!' she cried. 'I got two sisters, coming to Jigalong!'

And so it was. Molly, Gracie, and Daisy grew up in and around Jigalong, among their big Aboriginal family of mothers and aunties and uncles and grannies. They became as close as sisters, always together, living, sleeping, playing, walking in the bush, hunting for bush tucker . . .

\|/\|/\|/\|/

The white man called these children half-castes, children of Aboriginal mothers and white fathers. All over the country more and more half-caste children were being born, and the government was worried. Where did these children belong? To their black Aboriginal families? Or to the white man's world? The government decided that these children should go to school, where they would learn how to become domestic servants and farm workers. Two schools were started, one in the south-west, and one near Perth, called the Moore River Native Settlement. Aboriginal children all over Western Australia were taken away from their families and sent to these schools, to learn how to live like the white man.

The years passed, and the seasons came and went. Jigalong was a long way from anywhere, but government officers rode all over the country, looking for part-Aboriginal children. The arm of the law was long, and reached even to Jigalong. Notes were kept at the depots and the stations, reports and letters were written, orders were given . . .

> To Mr A. O. Neville
> Chief Protector of Aborigines, Perth
> The half-caste girls at Jigalong have a hard time with the other Aboriginal children here, who say unkind things about them. The girls need a better chance in life than they can get out here in the bush.
> Arthur T. Hungerford
> Superintendent, Jigalong Depot

> To Mr A. O. Neville
> Chief Protector of Aborigines, Perth
> There are three half-caste girls at Jigalong – Molly 14 years, Gracie 10 years, and Daisy, about 8 years. I think you should do something about them as they are running wild at Jigalong Depot.
> Mrs Chellow
> Manager, Murra Munda Station

To Constable Riggs
Marble Bar Station
Find the three half-caste girls, Molly, Gracie, and Daisy, at Jigalong and bring them in. They will be sent to the Moore River Native Settlement. Send them down by ship to Fremantle, and an officer will meet them there.
Mr A. O. Neville
Chief Protector of Aborigines, Perth

'Find the three half-caste girls at Jigalong and bring them in.'

2

Leaving Jigalong

IN JULY 1931 the rainy season was a good one. For the Mardu people in the Western Desert, this was the time for taking long walks in the bush, hunting for bush food, and cooking it over fires at night.

Molly and her two cousins enjoyed living in the bush. They picked yellow flowers from the trees, and put them in buckets of water to make a sweet drink. They ate girdi-girdi, a kind of kangaroo, and damper, a flat bread cooked in the hot ashes of the fire. The weather was beautiful – warm, but not too hot, with a deep blue sky behind the shiny, grey-green leaves of the trees. When the rains were over, the heat of the sun would burn the land brown and dry, but for now everything was bright and new and green. It was a good time.

Early one morning everybody was having a breakfast of damper and tea when the dogs began to bark.

'Shut up!' shouted Maude, throwing a stick at one of them.

The dogs went quiet, but soon began to bark again. All eyes turned to look through the trees, and there, on a low hill behind them, stood a tall white man, looking down at them. He wore a uniform, with a wide brown hat.

'Who's that?' said Granny Frinda, the girls' grandmother.

'It's that policeman from Marble Bar,' said Maude, staring at him. 'Riggs . . . Constable Riggs.'

The policeman began to walk down the hill towards them. He was holding a piece of paper in his hand.

Maude stood up, suddenly afraid. She knew what was going to happen. The last time she was at Jigalong Depot, Mr Hungerford the superintendent had warned her that the police were looking for the half-caste girls.

'I've come to take Molly, Gracie, and Daisy, the half-caste girls,' Riggs called out. He held the piece of paper higher in his hand, to show them. 'They have to go to school, at the Moore River Native Settlement. The law says so.'

The oldest man in the family, the grandfather, nodded to

'Get in the back,' said Riggs. 'Hurry up!
We've got a long way to go.'

show that he understood what Riggs was saying. Maude held Molly close to her, and began to cry.

'Come on, you girls,' Riggs ordered. 'Don't worry about taking anything. We'll pick up what you need at Jigalong.'

The three girls stood up, scared and miserable. They followed Riggs back up the hill, through the trees, to his car. Behind them they could hear their family crying, calling out the Mardu words of pain and grief.

When they reached the car, Riggs got in. The girls stood silently, too frightened to speak.

'Come on,' Riggs said. 'Get in the back. Hurry up! I want to get started. We've got a long way to go.'

He drove away slowly over the rocky ground. The family left the camp at once, and began walking back to Jigalong. They went quickly, but Riggs was already driving away when they came near the depot.

Mr Hungerford came out to talk to them.

'Why they take our girls away?' Maude shouted. 'Why? Why? Why?' She was angry and crying at the same time.

'It's the law, Maude, you know that,' said Mr Hungerford. 'It's to give the girls a better chance, send them to school, so they can make a good life for themselves.'

Alf Fields, Gracie's white father, was standing silently near the side of the depot building. Gracie's mother Lilly saw him and ran over to him. She screamed at him in two languages, and beat his chest with her small hands.

'Why didn't you stop them?' she cried out.

'I couldn't,' said Alf Fields. 'The policeman was just doing his job – doing what the law tells him to do. If I try to stop him, they'll put me in prison.'

Lilly wasn't listening. 'You're a white man too,' she cried. 'They'll listen to you. Go and talk to them.'

'I'm sorry,' he said sadly. 'There's nothing I can do. I can't stop the government taking our daughter away from us.'

Lilly turned away. Then she fell to the ground, and began to shout and cry. 'Worrah! Worrah! Worrah!'

Old Granny Frinda and the other women joined in.

'Aieee, aieee! They have taken our little ones away! Aieee, aieee, aieee . . .'

Long after the car had disappeared, the cries of the Mardu women rang out over the desert, calling for their daughters and their granddaughters to come back to them.

卅/卅卅

The journey took several days. First they went north, a long day driving on dirt roads full of holes. Once or twice Constable Riggs shouted over the noise of the car engine:

'You girls alright back there?'

But those were the only words he spoke. He did not tell them where they were going, or what would happen next. By the end of the day the girls were too tired to cry, and they spoke only in whispers to each other, sitting close together on the back seat. Sometimes they slept, then woke again, to stare out of the car windows, full of fear for the future.

When they arrived at Marble Bar, it was late and the sky was black with rain clouds. They slept the night in the police station there, and the next day a different policeman took them by train to Port Hedland on the north coast. They went by car from the railway station down to the ship.

Children who have lived all their lives in the Western Desert have never seen the sea. Gracie and Daisy stared out of the car window at the ship.

'We going on that?' whispered Gracie.

The policeman laughed at their scared faces. 'Yes, you're going down to Fremantle by ship. You'll like it, you'll see.'

For five days they sailed down the coast of Western Australia, and when they stopped being scared by the movement of the sea, the girls did enjoy it. It was warm and sunny, and the people on the ship were kind to them. One of

Gracie and Daisy stared at the ship.
'We going on that?' whispered Gracie.

the women took care of them, and they became friendly with George, a sailor, who taught them the English names of the stars and told them about his travels in far-away countries.

As they sailed south, the weather changed, and when they landed in Fremantle, it was wet and cold and grey.

Fremantle frightened them. It was so big, so noisy, so crowded. They had never seen so many white men in one place before. They were driven to Perth, which was bigger and noisier and even more frightening. And all the time there were new people meeting them, taking them here, taking them there, talking to them, asking questions.

'We're from Jigalong,' Molly would say to all these strange new faces looking down at them.

Jigalong was home. Jigalong was where their mothers were. Jigalong was a long, long way away . . .

††/††††

At last they arrived at Moore River Native Settlement. In the government plan, this was going to be their home for several years. Here they would learn to be European, learn the white man's ways, learn to forget their own people and the wide, empty, beautiful Western Desert where they were born.

It was dark when the car stopped. They got out, and a woman came towards them through the rain.

'Come with me,' she said. 'I'm Miss Evans, I take care of the girls here. I'll take you to your dormitory. This way.'

They followed her to a wooden building, and watched as she unlocked the big padlocks on the door. Inside they saw a long room, full of beds with shapes under grey blankets.

Miss Evans showed them some empty beds near one wall. 'There are your beds. Oh, and for a toilet, you use one of those buckets in the bathroom.' Then she went away.

Molly, Daisy, and Gracie lay down on the hard beds, under the thin blankets. They were shaking with cold.

After a while, Gracie whispered to Molly, 'Dgudu, I can't sleep. I'm so cold.' She and Daisy were younger than Molly, so they called her Dgudu, older sister, because that was the usual Mardu way to speak to an older sister-cousin.

'Bring your blanket and sleep in my bed,' Molly whispered.

Then Daisy sat up and whispered, 'I'm cold too, Dgudu.'

'You can sleep on my other side,' Molly said. 'Come on.'

For the rest of the night the three of them lay close in the same bed, keeping warm. They were tired, and slept deeply.

To Constable Riggs
Marble Bar Station
The three girls from Jigalong have arrived safely at Moore River. They seem very scared, and need watching to stop them running away. We have seen this in other children when they first arrive, but have always found that they soon calm down and accept their new life here.
Mr A. O. Neville
Chief Protector of Aborigines, Perth
4 August 1931

3

Learning the white man's ways

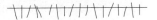

VERY EARLY NEXT morning the three girls were woken by a strange voice shouting loudly,

'Come on, girls, wake up, wake up!'

It was Miss Evans. She went round the room, pulling the blankets off the beds and shaking the girls awake. When she came to Molly's bed, she stared at the three girls lying there.

'Ah yes . . . the new girls. Alright, make your beds, then get some breakfast. The others will show you where to go.'

Making the beds was easy – you just pulled the blanket straight. There were no sheets. When visitors came to Moore River, sheets were put on the beds, to look good. But after the visitors had gone, the sheets were taken away again.

One of the bigger girls came over to them. 'I'm Martha Jones,' she said. 'I'm from Port Hedland. I've been here one year now. I can show you round, if you like.'

Martha was friendly, and full of useful information. The girls from Jigalong liked her at once.

A loud bell sounded somewhere. 'That's the breakfast bell,' said Martha. 'We have to hurry, or the tea will be cold.'

They went outside. They could see the boys' dormitory and children running across to another building. There was thin sunlight, but the air was cold. 'It's not so bad here once you know the place,' Martha told them.

'I don't like this place,' Molly thought. 'It's like a prison.'

Molly said nothing. She stood still and stared across at other dormitory buildings, saw the metal bars across all the windows, the big padlocks on all the doors.

'I don't like this place,' she thought. 'It's like a prison. They lock you up at night time, and let you out in the morning.'

After breakfast, the new girls were sent to the washroom where a nurse washed them from head to foot in cold water. They were given new white dresses to wear, and shoes.

The lunch was just as bad as the breakfast. 'The food never gets any better,' said Martha. 'We get meat sometimes at

dinner, but mostly we get soup with not much meat in it.'
They walked together back to the dormitory. 'Do you want
to come for a walk?' Martha asked. 'I can show you the river
if you like. Lots of girls go down there to play.'

With another girl called Polly they walked behind the
dormitory, passed a kind of field where some of the boys
were playing a ball game, and climbed down the track to the
river. With the recent rains the river was high, its deep brown
waters hurrying noisily between the rocks. There were tall
trees, their tops waving in the wind, small trees with bright
pink flowers, and bushes covered with golden flowers.

It was a beautiful place, but the trees and the flowers were
all strange to Molly. Her heart ached for home, for the red
earth and the dry salt lakes and the river beds of the Western
Desert, for the trees and bushes and flowers that she knew.

As they walked back into the settlement, they passed a
small square building on the corner, and heard a voice calling.

'Hey, who's out there?'

'It's me, Polly, with Martha, and three new girls.'

'Can you tell my sister to bring me some damper and some
tea?' the girl's voice said. She sounded very unhappy.

'Yeah, I tell her,' Polly promised.

'What's that place?' asked Molly. There was one small
window with bars, high on one wall.

'It's the punishment building,' said Martha. 'We call it
the "boob". Poor Violet is in there for two days, because she
said bad words to Miss Morgan, the teacher. But she's lucky.'

'Lucky? Why's she lucky?' Gracie said.

'You should see the girls who were locked up for running away,' Polly said. 'They were in the "boob" for seven days, with just bread and water. They had all their hair cut right off, and they were beaten too. It was terrible.'

'Oh!' Daisy whispered, her eyes wide with fear.

'How far did they get?' asked Molly.

'Not very far. Only to the railway line south of Mogumber,' Martha said. 'The trains slow down there, and they were going to jump on a train. But the black tracker found them there.' Martha's voice became angry. 'And he made them walk all the way back here, without stopping, while he rode behind them on his horse, like a white policeman.'

There was a little silence for a while.

Then Molly asked, 'Has anyone ever escaped? Really escaped, I mean, got away and got back to their home?'

'No. Lots of people have tried to run away, but that black tracker has always caught them and brought them back. Then they get beaten and locked up in the "boob". Sometimes they're in there for fourteen days.'

The girls walked on in silence along the main road through the settlement. They had passed the church when Martha stopped suddenly.

'Look,' she said, 'look over there. There's that black tracker I was telling you about. His name's Moodoo.'

The girls turned to look, and saw a tall thin man in a black jacket. He passed them, his face unsmiling. Daisy hid her face in Molly's skirt as he passed.

At dinner it was the same uninteresting food – sweet milky

'There's that black tracker I was telling you about.'

tea, bread, and some kind of vegetable soup with small pieces of grey meat. Molly put several pieces of bread in her pockets, and whispered to Gracie and Daisy,

'You take some too. Fill your pockets. For later.'

After dinner everybody ran back to the dormitories because it was beginning to rain hard. The girls sat or lay on the beds, the younger ones listening to the older ones telling stories, laughing, talking about their hopes for the future. 'When I get back home . . .' were words that were often said, but very few of these girls would ever see their homes again. The government would send them to work as servants in farms and depots hundreds of miles from their homes.

Molly, Daisy, and Gracie sat together on one bed, talking in their own Mardu language.

'You girls can't talk that language here, you know,' a voice warned from another bed. 'You gotta forget it and talk English all the time.'

The Jigalong girls stared at the speaker in surprise.

'It's true,' said Martha. 'I had to do the same. They tell everyone that when they go to school the first time.'

Molly could not believe it. 'We can't talk in our own language?' she whispered. 'That's awful.'

'We know it's awful,' Martha said. 'But we got over it.'

Soon Miss Evans came to put the lights out and lock the doors. Molly lay there in the darkness, listening to the keys turning in the big padlocks.

'We can't live in this place,' she whispered to herself. 'We're gunna get away from here, we're gunna go home, home to Jigalong.'

†//†††††

They were woken at six o'clock the next morning. Molly ran to the window and looked out. The sky was dark and grey.

'More rain coming,' thought Molly, and smiled.

After breakfast, everybody returned to the dormitory to get ready for school. Soon afterwards, the school bell sounded.

'Come on,' Martha said to Molly. 'The bell's gone. Don't be late on your first day of school.'

19

'Yes, alright, but we gotta empty the toilet bucket first.'

'I'll wait for you then,' said Martha.

'No, don't wait,' said Molly softly. 'We'll follow you, we know where the school is.'

'Alright, we'll go along. Come on, Polly.' And Martha left.

When all the girls had left, Molly turned to Gracie and Daisy. 'We're not going to school,' she whispered. 'Get your bags. We're going home to Jigalong.'

The two younger girls stared at her, confused and scared. 'What?' said Gracie.

Daisy looked frightened. 'But Dgudu . . . How we gunna find our way back to Jigalong? It's a long way.'

Molly and Daisy looked carefully round the corner of the building.

'I know it's a long way, but it's easy,' said Molly. 'We'll find the rabbit-proof fence and follow it home.'

'We gunna walk all the way?' said Daisy.

'Yes,' said Molly. ' My daddy worked on the fence. He was an inspector, alright? He told me about the fence. It goes all the way from the south to the north. We just gotta find it.'

The younger girls usually did what their big sister told them to, so they ran to get their white cotton bags. There was not much in them – a hairbrush, a little mirror, a few pieces of dry bread. They left the dormitory, carrying the toilet bucket between them, and walked down to the washroom. When they came out, Molly looked carefully round the corner of the building. Daisy looked too, holding on to Molly's skirt.

There was nobody around. The road through the settlement was empty. Molly turned to the other two.

'Now!' she whispered. 'Run! Follow me!'

And away they went, down through the trees towards the river, running like the wind. They ran by the river for two hours, looking for a place to cross. After the rain the ground was soft and wet, and it was hard work, pushing through the thick bushes. At last they found a good place. A tree had fallen across a narrow part of the river, making a bridge.

When they had crossed to the other side, Molly turned to Gracie and Daisy. 'We go north now, all the way home.'

4

Walking north

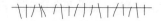

HOW DO YOU keep travelling north on a grey day when you can't see the sun, and you don't have a map?

Molly did not need a map. She had lived all her life in the bush, and although the land here in the south was strange to her, she knew which way to go.

Leaving the river behind them, they began to cross some low hills, thickly covered with acacia bushes. The spines of the acacia leaves cut their bare legs, but the girls did not stop. Soon it began to rain.

'We got no coats,' said Gracie. 'We gunna get so wet.'

'Never mind!' Molly said happily. 'Rain is good! Think about that black tracker – he can't follow our tracks now because the rain will wash them all away.'

With that happy thought they went on walking through the rain, through woodlands and open ground, over hills, and down valleys. When it began to get dark, Molly stopped to look around.

'We gotta find a good, safe place to make a camp for the night,' she said. 'See that little hill down there, in that valley. It's full of rabbit holes. We'll dig a hole for us, make it big enough for three of us.'

'We gunna sleep in the ground like rabbits?' said Grace.

'Nobody gunna look in a rabbit hole for us,' Molly said.

Daisy laughed. 'No, nobody will find us in there.'

They found an old, unused hole, and side by side they dug with their hands to make it big enough for the three of them. Molly had chosen a hole that faced east, because she had noticed that the rain always came from the west.

They ate some of their dry bread, drank water from a little river in the valley, and climbed into their rabbit hole. It was crowded, but it was warm and dry and safe. They slept deeply.

The next morning, they were woken by the sound of rabbits running all around them. They thought hungrily about breakfast – a nice fat rabbit cooking over a fire.

Gracie got up, chased a rabbit, caught it, and killed it.

'What did you do that for?' said Molly angrily. 'We got no matches to make a fire to cook it.'

'Well, I'm hungry,' Gracie said miserably. She threw the dead rabbit away, and for breakfast they had lots of cool water from the river, and hard dry bread from their bags. It was the second meal of their journey.

Gracie was still miserable. 'Dgudu, we gotta go back to the settlement. We gunna die out here. Please, let's go back.'

'You want to go back to the settlement?' said Molly angrily. 'You heard what they'll do to us. They'll cut our hair off, give us a big beating, and lock us up in that prison place.'

Daisy stood silently, watching them and listening.

'You want to go back, you're mad,' Molly said. 'We three came together, and we're going home together. So let's go.'

But Gracie refused to move. 'I'm hungry, Dgudu. I want some meat, not just bread and water.'

23

Molly walked back to Gracie and put her arm round her shoulder. 'Don't worry, we gunna find something to eat, you'll see,' she said gently. 'This country's different from ours, so we gotta learn to find their bush tucker, that's all. Come on, let's go along now.'

And so on they went, walking north under a grey sky, and with a cold wind blowing through their thin cotton dresses. They could not stop thinking about a meal of meat, hot damper, and sweet tea.

They came to another river, but this one was shallow and

They stopped to listen, looking fearfully around them.

24

easy to walk through. Halfway across they heard voices, and stopped to listen, looking fearfully around them.

Men's voices, coming towards them.

'Quick, hide!' said Molly. She pulled her young sisters behind a thick bush, and pushed them to the ground.

The voices came closer – speaking Mardu words. Molly looked out. It was two Mardu men returning from a hunting trip, carrying a large, cooked kangaroo. They were very surprised when the three girls ran out to meet them.

'We're from Marble Bar,' the older of the two men said. 'Where are you girls going?'

'We're running away from the settlement,' said Molly. 'Going home to Jigalong.'

'Well, you girls want to be careful,' said the younger man. 'I hear they've got a Mardu policeman, a tracker. He finds runaways and takes them back to the settlement.'

'He can't follow us in the rain,' said Molly.

The men gave them a cooked kangaroo tail, a box of matches, and a little box of salt. They shook hands with the girls and said goodbye. 'Don't forget now, go quickly. That Mardu tracker will be out looking for you soon.'

They went on walking until it began to get dark. Then they built themselves a shelter for the night, with branches of trees and bushes. They found lots of wood, and made a fire in a hole in the ground in the middle of their shelter. That night they ate kangaroo tail, the last piece of bread, and drank rain water. Then they slept, warm and comfortable around the fire in their little shelter.

The next morning they finished the kangaroo tail, covered up the fire hole, and moved on. The rain had stopped, but there were more dark rain clouds in the west.

By midday they were feeling very hungry again. Gracie walked more and more slowly. Once she fell down, and just lay there, saying, 'We gunna die, we got nothing to eat.'

Molly became angry. 'Oh, shut up,' she said. She pulled Gracie to her feet. 'We gotta hurry. We gotta keep walking.'

Late in the afternoon Molly gave a sudden shout. 'Look over there,' she called excitedly.

It was another small hill full of rabbit holes.

'We sleeping in a rabbit hole again, Dgudu?' said Gracie.

'No. We gunna catch some rabbits. And eat them.'

And they did. Two fat rabbits were cooked over their fire that night; one was eaten, and the other saved for breakfast.

The fourth day began bright and clear, and after a breakfast of cold rabbit, they began walking again. The land was drier here, and the trees and bushes different. Sometimes they came to open grassland among the trees, but there were still plenty of thick bushes to hide under.

Once they saw two big black kangaroos fighting. They watched, scared, from behind some bushes.

'They're standing up and fighting like men,' Molly said.

'I'm frightened, Dgudu,' said Gracie.

'Me too, Dgudu,' said Daisy, holding on to Molly's dress.

Molly did not feel too brave herself. 'We'll walk round them,' she said. 'Make a big circle. They won't see us.'

Later in the morning they stopped for a rest, sitting on a

fallen tree. Everything seemed very peaceful until Molly suddenly jumped to her feet.

'Quick! Run to that big tree over there. Come on, hurry!'

The younger girls had no time to ask what was happening because Molly was shouting at them to climb the tree and lie still along the branches. They all did that, and lay there waiting and listening. And then the two younger girls heard it too.

It was a plane, a search plane. Was it out looking for them, the runaway girls from the settlement? They lay along their branches without moving, hidden by the leaves of the tree, while the plane circled above them. At last it went away, but the girls stayed still for some time, afraid that it would return.

When they climbed back down, they were still worried, and walked along as fast as they could, keeping close to the trees. They did not notice the weather until heavy rain began to fall, and soon they were wet to the skin, cold and miserable.

Then they heard sounds they knew – chickens squawking, dogs barking, a gate banging. Somewhere nearby was a farmhouse. Then they saw it, in the valley just below them.

When your stomach has been empty all day, you have to do something about it. Molly turned to the other two.

'Go down there and ask the woman for something to eat. Hurry up. I'll wait here, and watch.'

5
Finding the fence

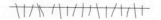

DAISY AND GRACIE were too hungry to feel afraid. They left Molly sitting behind a big tree, and slowly walked down to the farmhouse. The dogs barked at them, but the girls opened the gate and went in.

On the verandah in front of the farmhouse a little girl of about four years was playing. She saw them and called out to them, then ran to open the house door.

'Mummy,' she shouted, 'there's two girls outside and they're all wet.'

Daisy and Gracie stood on the verandah, waiting, while the rain water ran off their clothes onto the wooden floor.

A woman came to the door and looked at them.

'Are you the runaways from the settlement?'

'Yes.'

'Where's the other one?'

'She's outside,' said Gracie. 'Near that big tree.'

'Go and tell her to come inside and dry herself. I'll make you all something to eat.'

The woman's name was Mrs Flanagan. The superintendent at the Moore River Settlement had phoned a few days ago, asking her to watch out for the runaway half-castes.

'Where are you girls going?' she asked, when all three of them were sitting in her warm, dry kitchen.

'We're gunna find the rabbit-proof fence,' Molly said. 'Follow it home to Jigalong.'

'Well, you're going in the wrong direction,' said Mrs Flanagan. 'The rabbit-proof fence isn't north from here, it's east. If you go north, you'll come to the coast at Geraldton. You want to go east towards Wubin.'

She made them some thick meat and tomato sandwiches, which they ate in seconds, they were so hungry. Then she gave them big pieces of fruit cake and cups of sweet, milky tea. Soon they were feeling warm and sleepy.

When they had eaten enough, Mrs Flanagan filled some brown paper bags with tea leaves, sugar, salt, flour, a big piece of cold meat, some bread, and a fruit cake. She added three billycans for water.

'You'll need these to make your tea in,' she said. 'Now, come with me, and I'll get you some coats to wear.'

Outside in a storeroom she found some old army coats. 'Here, take these. They'll keep you warm, and they'll keep some of the rain out.'

She stood on her verandah watching them as they walked away into the trees. 'Those girls are too young to walk around in the bush on their own,' she thought. 'They'll die for sure. I'll have to report them before they get lost.'

She went back inside to phone the superintendent. 'I'm doing the right thing, I'm sure I am,' she said to herself. 'Those girls won't get any further than other runaways. They always get caught.'

╫╫╫╫╫

But Molly was not like other runaways. She knew much more about the bush than other Mardu girls of her age, and she had a clear, fixed plan in her head. She and her sister-cousins were going home to Jigalong, and nobody was going to stop them.

As they walked away, she turned in a north-east direction and said to Gracie and Daisy, 'I made a mistake, telling that woman where we're going. She knows we're going east. So we don't go east. We go this way.'

'Is she gunna report us?' asked Daisy, worried.

'Maybe,' Molly said. 'Never mind. We'll make sure no tracker can follow us.'

The girls stepped carefully from stone to stone,
leaving no footprints on the dusty ground.

They walked quickly on for several kilometres until it began to get dark. The land was more open here, with fewer good hiding-places, but they found some thick bushes and built a shelter under them. They dug a hole for a fire in the centre of the shelter, collected some dry wood and leaves, and soon they were warm and comfortable round their fire, eating cold meat and fruit cake, and drinking hot sweet tea.

The next morning the sky was clear. After some hot tea they covered their fire hole and pulled down the shelter.

'Now,' said Molly, 'we can go east. Follow me. Watch.'

Their route lay over some open ground which was covered in big stones. Molly stepped carefully from stone to stone, never letting her feet touch the dusty ground. Gracie and Daisy followed her, doing the same. They went quite a long way like this, leaving no footprints for a tracker to find.

As the three girls travelled east, news of their escape was travelling all over the country. On 11th August 1931 this notice appeared in the *West Australian* newspaper.

MISSING ABORIGINAL GIRLS

The Chief Protector of Aborigines, Mr Neville, is worried about three native girls, from eight to fourteen years old, who ran away from Moore River Native Settlement several days ago. 'We have been searching for the children for days,' said Mr Neville, 'and the only thing we found is a dead rabbit which they had tried to eat. If anybody sees them, please inform me at once. It is not safe for them to be out in the bush on their own.'

Mrs Flanagan was not the only person with news of the runaways. Three days after the newspaper report the police station at Dalwallinu sent this to Mr Neville:

Report from Mr D. Lyons, farmer
The three native girls called at my farm on Saturday. I gave them some food, then they left, going east towards Burakin. I asked them where they had come from, but they would not tell me. They wore old army coats of some kind.

Other farmers sent in news, messages went backwards and forwards, reports went to and from police stations . . . but Molly, Gracie, and Daisy just went on walking. They did not know that the police search parties were sometimes only a few days behind them.

On they went, now travelling through farmlands and fields of sheep or cattle. They found a farmhouse every few days, and followed the same plan as before. The younger girls went in and asked for food while Molly hid outside, where she could watch them. Thankfully, food was never refused.

They took great care now when they went to a farmhouse. They came to it from one direction and pretended to leave in the opposite direction. Then they would do a full circle round the farmhouse, making sure nobody was following them, and go back and continue along their usual route.

They were also careful with their cooking fire at night, always digging a hole where the fire could burn unseen. In the morning they covered the ashes of the fire, and filled in the hole. Nothing was left to show where they had been.

The three girls had now been on the run for over a month, and the land began to feel more like home. They could recognize some of the trees and bushes, and the colour of the earth was nearly the same red as at Jigalong.

Walking had become difficult for them. The cuts on their legs from acacia bushes had become red and angry-looking sores, and were painful to touch.

'My legs hurt, Dgudu,' Gracie said one day. 'I can't walk.'

Daisy was also miserable. 'My legs hurt too,' she said.

'Well, so do mine,' said Molly, 'but we can't stop. We gotta walk further. I'll carry Daisy for a bit, then have a rest, then I'll carry you.'

'Alright,' said Gracie.

This made them slower, but still they went on walking. When it was Molly's turn to have a rest from carrying them, the younger sisters sometimes rode on each other's backs. The sores on their legs did not get any better, and their legs ached all the time.

But they went on walking.

When they could catch them, they ate birds, rabbits, and lizards. When they were given flour by women on the farms, they made their own damper and cooked it in hot ashes.

One day, under a hot midday sun, Daisy and Gracie heard an excited shout from Molly, who was walking ahead of them.

'I've found it! Here it is. Come and look,' she shouted, laughing and waving her arms.

'What is it?' said Gracie. 'Why are you shouting?'

'I've found it! I've found the rabbit-proof fence!'

Gracie and Daisy came to look.

'But what's so special about this fence, Dgudu?' Daisy said. 'How do you know it's the rabbit-proof fence?'

'Because it's straight, see,' Molly said. 'And they've cut down the bushes on both sides. My father told me all about it.' She put both hands on the fence and added softly, 'And it's gunna take us all the way home to Jigalong.'

'This fence is gunna take us all the way home to Jigalong.'

6

Hiding from the white man

FINDING THE FENCE was a great moment in the long walk. It was a landmark for the Mardudjara people of the Western Desert, and for the three runaway girls the fence was a part of their own world. It belonged to their own place, the place that they were trying so hard to get back to.

'We're nearly home,' Molly said. 'It gunna be easy now. We just gunna walk alongside the fence all the way to Jigalong.'

Molly did not realize that they were not 'nearly home'. They were less than halfway, and still had more than eight hundred kilometres to walk. But the fence gave the girls hope; it was like meeting a long-lost friend – a friend that would show them the way home.

Perhaps the girls had found a friend in the rabbit-proof fence, but their enemies were closing in on them. Down in Perth, Mr Neville, Chief Protector of Aborigines, sent a telegram to the police station in Geraldton.

IT WILL LOOK BAD FOR THE GOVERNMENT IF THESE GIRLS ARE NOT CAUGHT. SPEND THE MONEY NEEDED AND FIND AND CATCH THEM AS SOON AS POSSIBLE.

The Inspector in Geraldton sent orders to constables in police stations near and far. Keep looking for the runaways. Ask farmers and station workers to watch out for them. Send reports in quickly, by telephone or telegram.

Most people now knew about the three half-caste girls in their old army coats walking through the bush. But by the time a report reached a police station, Molly, Daisy, and Gracie had already moved on. They were walking about thirty kilometres every day, and the police could never catch up with them.

┼┼┼┼┼┼┼

The day after finding the fence, the girls came to a clearing in the acacia bushes. Daisy looked around her.

'Look, Dgudu,' she said. 'Lots of goanna holes here. Maybe we can catch one?'

Goannas are a kind of lizard and, as usual, the girls were hungry. Molly stopped to look, but at that moment they heard a man's voice shouting.

'Hey, you girls!'

They turned, and saw an Aboriginal man riding a bicycle down the track along the fence. At once they ran back into the thickest acacia bushes and threw themselves down on the ground to hide.

'Don't run away. I want to talk to you,' the man shouted. They looked out carefully between the bushes, and saw the man still on the track, holding something in one hand. 'Look,' he shouted, 'I've got some food to give you. See. Come on, don't be frightened.'

'I'm hungry, Dgudu,' whispered Gracie.

They were all hungry, hungry from morning to night, and their need for food was stronger than their fear.

They sat on the ground in the clearing, and the man gave

them cold meat and bread from his lunch box. He also gave them a box of matches.

'My name's Don,' he said. 'What are you called?'

No answer.

Don tried again. 'Where are you going?' he asked.

'We gunna follow the railway line to Wiluna,' lied Molly. She stood up, still eating her piece of bread. 'We're going now. Come on,' she said to the younger girls. Gracie and Daisy stood up and followed her, still eating.

Don Willocks watched them walk away. After a while they stopped, and the smallest girl climbed on the back of the biggest girl. They did not look back at him and soon they had disappeared into the desert.

Don Willocks reported this meeting to his employer, who reported it to Constable Larsen at Yalgoo Station. Larsen telephoned Inspector Simpson in Geraldton.

The search began again. Moodoo, the black tracker from Moore River Settlement, was sent up to help, and on 5th September he and Constable Larsen drove up to Pindathuna to pick up Don Willocks. Then they went on up to the rabbit-proof fence, where Don had seen the girls.

But rain the night before had washed away the tracks. The searchers continued along the fence, looking for tracks as they went. When darkness came, they made a camp, and the next morning at first light they started again. Almost at once, Moodoo found some tracks, but very soon afterwards the tracks disappeared again. They went twenty-eight kilometres north of Dalgaranga Station, but Moodoo found no more

Moodoo found no more tracks.

tracks, and on 7th September the search party returned to Yalgoo.

They did not know that the three runaways had climbed over the fence and gone back to look for some bush tucker. They returned a different way, joining the fence further up.

††ⵏ†ⵏ††

To Inspector Simpson
Police Station, Geraldton
We believe these girls are following the rabbit-proof fence north. They were probably frightened by seeing Willocks near Pindathuna, and have been travelling very fast, about sixty kilometres in two days. They will have to slow down soon – they cannot keep walking distances like that every day. Perhaps somebody can wait at the fence near Gum Creek; the girls will have to pass that way if they are following the fence.
Constable Larsen
Yalgoo Station

To Mr A. O. Neville
Chief Protector of Aborigines, Perth
If we do not catch these girls, I am afraid that they will have a very bad time after they pass Gum Creek on the old Nannine–Wiluna Road. We are sure that the girls will keep following the rabbit-proof fence. At this time of year there is plenty of water and food in the bush, but there will be much less as the girls get into the desert further north, and I fear for their safety.
Inspector Simpson
Police Station, Geraldton

Molly, Daisy, and Gracie were also afraid for their safety. After meeting Don Willocks, they knew that everybody was looking for them. They knew that at any time of the day or night the police could find them and catch them – and send them back to Moore River Settlement.

They slept for only a few hours every night, moving on at first light every morning. They lived on bush tucker and water. They did not go near any farmhouses, and although the nights were still cold, they lit no fires.

One evening in a clearing close to the fence the girls saw some young birds on the ground. They chased and caught a bird each, then found a place where they could light a fire safely and not be seen. They cooked the birds and made some damper with some of the flour they still had left. After supper they found a place to sleep under some thick bushes.

That night Molly dreamed. A policeman and the black tracker were chasing her and her sisters. She could see them riding beside the fence on grey horses, coming towards them from the north. They were coming closer and closer . . . and she woke up, shaking with fear.

And heard them. It wasn't a dream after all, it was real. There were horses coming towards them.

Quickly, Molly shook the other two awake. 'Keep still. Don't make a sound,' she whispered. 'I can hear horses. I think it's a policeman and that Mardu tracker.'

The girls lay on their stomachs, as still and as silent as frightened rabbits, listening. The horses came closer, and passed slowly by them. Voices were heard, laughing.

Molly carefully sat up and looked. 'Not policemen,' she whispered thankfully. 'Just farm workers.'

Light was now appearing in the eastern sky, so they got up and started walking. There was a piece of damper left from the night before, and they ate it as they walked.

As they followed the fence north-east, they came to a road going north. They could see something moving on the road, and in the distance the buildings of a town.

'Get down!' whispered Molly quickly. 'We gotta wait till the road is clear. Then we can cross it.'

They crouched together on the ground, keeping their heads low, watching the road from behind some acacia bushes. They saw a car go by, and two people on bicycles.

'What town is that, Dgudu?' said Daisy.

They crouched together on the ground, keeping their heads low.

'Meekatharra, I think,' said Molly.

'Let's go into the town, Dgudu,' said Gracie. 'We can ask somebody to give us food for the road.'

'No,' Molly said. 'There'll be policemen in that town.'

'That old lady, Minnie, she lives in Meekatharra,' said Gracie. 'You know, the one that used to be on Ethel Creek Station.'

'No! The police gunna pick us up and send us back to Moore River. You know that.'

Daisy said nothing. Molly and Gracie often argued, and Daisy didn't worry about it any more.

Gracie went on trying. 'She's the one married to that old man from Nullagine. She'll help us, I know she will.'

'No!' said Molly angrily. 'We go around Meekatharra. Come on – we can cross the road now. Hurry!'

╫╱╫╫╫╱

A week later Constable Penn of the Meekatharra police station, with a tracker called Jacky, drove along the Nannine to Meekatharra road to the place where the rabbit-proof fence crossed it. They searched along the fence, looking for tracks on both sides of it, but found nothing. They went quite a long way into rough country, made a camp near the fence, and waited there for two days, watching for the runaways.

But the runaways never walked too close to the fence, because of leaving tracks that would be easy to find. And they had passed that place several days ago, and were already a long way north of it. Although they were hungry and tired, although they had painful sores on their legs, they were still

They waited there for two days, watching for the runaways.

walking between twenty-five and thirty kilometres a day.
Molly carried Daisy on her back when Daisy was too tired to
walk. Sometimes she carried Gracie. Sometimes she and
Gracie carried Daisy between them.

They were now in the desert land where they had been
born. They knew where to find water. They knew the trees
where birds made their nests. They knew how to find the
holes where the goannas lived, and how to catch them.

And they were getting closer to home every day.

7
Losing Gracie

A FEW DAYS later, early in the morning, the girls crossed the railway line near Mount Russel station. They could see the station not far away, and some people working there.

Gracie stood still and stared at them. 'I'm going to the station, to talk to those people,' she said suddenly.

'Why? What you gunna do?' asked Molly.

But Gracie was already walking away from them.

'Where's she going?' asked Daisy. She held on to Molly's coat with both hands. 'Tell her to come back, Dgudu.'

Gracie was already too far away and Molly did not want to shout. She and Daisy hid behind some bushes, and waited.

Fifteen minutes later Gracie came back, looking excited and happy. She crouched down next to them.

'That woman, the muda-muda one working down there' – Gracie waved her arm in the direction of the station – 'she told me that my mummy left Jigalong and is living in Wiluna. I can get the train to Wiluna. The muda-muda woman says I can go with her when the train comes.'

Molly stared at her. 'We come all this way,' she whispered, 'and now you're gunna let them get you . . . send you back to Moore River. You're mad.'

Gracie stood up. 'No,' she said, 'no. I can't walk any more, Dgudu. I'm tired. I'm going to my mummy in Wiluna.'

*'I can't walk any more, Dgudu,' said Gracie. 'I'm tired.
I'm going to my mummy in Wiluna.'*

'But maybe she's not there any more,' Molly said. 'Maybe she's gone some other place that you don't know. Maybe this muda-muda woman is lying.'

'You gotta come with us,' said Daisy. 'Your mummy – she'll come and find you at Jigalong.'

'No,' said Gracie. 'I'm going to Wiluna. Jigalong still a long way from here. I can get the train to Wiluna.'

'Yes, but . . . there's lots of people in Wiluna,' Molly said unhappily. 'Somebody's gunna see you there, report you to the police. Then they're gunna send you back to Moore River . . . You want to go back to that place?'

Gracie turned her face away from them.

'Come back to Jigalong,' Daisy said. 'Come with us, Gracie. You go to Wiluna, you get caught.'

'I'm not gunna walk any more. I'm tired,' Gracie said.

Molly tried again. 'Gracie, listen. It's not safe to go to Wiluna. Jigalong is right out in the desert, the police don't come there often, and we can hide in the bush any time.'

'Jigalong too far,' Gracie said. She took a step away from them. 'I'm going to see my mummy.' She took another step. 'I'm going to Wiluna.'

She turned and walked away from them, down towards the station.

Molly stared after her, with tears in her eyes. 'She gunna get caught,' she whispered, 'she gunna get caught.'

Daisy moved closer to her sister, and Molly put her arm round her. With her other hand, she covered her eyes, and began to cry, the tears running down between her fingers.

'Maybe we wait a bit, Dgudu?' said Daisy. 'Maybe Gracie'll come back? Decide to go to Jigalong with us?'

Molly said nothing, and the tears continued to run down between her fingers. High above them in the sky, a great bird circled lazily on the hot wind, its long sad cry ringing through the desert air.

After a while Molly and Daisy got up. They went back to the rabbit-proof fence and began to follow it north again, walking away hand in hand into the desert.

By midday on the day that they lost Gracie, it had become very hot – the hottest day since their escape from Moore

Molly and Daisy began to follow the fence north again, walking away hand in hand into the desert.

River. Molly and Daisy threw away their army coats, knowing that they would not need them again. But they did need water. They found a little river bed which was almost dry, but had just enough water for them to have a drink and fill their billycans. This would give them enough water until they found one of the wells along the old cattle route.

After a few hours they came to a dry salt lake. It lay before them, a great wide place of white salt. Daisy stopped.

'My legs hurt, Dgudu.'

'Alright, I'll carry you to the other side.'

Molly picked Daisy up and began to walk across the salt. The sun burned down, but desert heat was nothing new to these Mardu girls, and Molly just went on walking.

'Not far now,' she whispered. 'We'll have a rest soon.'

They got to the other side, and Molly put Daisy down. She was very tired. Tired from the long weeks of walking, tired from the crying and the heartache of losing Gracie.

'I gotta sleep for a bit,' she said to Daisy. 'There's some trees over there. We'll go there.'

'Alright, Dgudu,' said Daisy. 'You sleep, and I'll look for bush tucker.'

Molly lay down, and was asleep in seconds. Daisy looked around for a while and then, seeing a bird's nest in a tree, climbed up the tree and found four young birds in the nest. She caught and killed three of them, one by one, but as she was climbing down, she fell and banged her knee on a rock. Her knee was not badly hurt, but the pain made her angry.

'Ow!' she shouted. 'Ow, ow, ow!'

Suddenly she heard a man's voice calling behind her.
'Hey, where's your big sister?'

Daisy turned and saw a young man, a muda-muda in cattle worker clothes, standing on a little rocky hill, watching her. His horse was tied to a tree nearby.

The sun burned down, but desert heat was nothing new to these Mardu girls, and Molly just went on walking.

'I said, where's your big sister?' he shouted at her. 'Tell her to come here to me. I want her. I heard about you girls, you ran away from that settlement, Moore River.'

He laughed unpleasantly and began to walk towards her. Daisy, frightened and angry, screamed at him in English and Mardu, telling him to go away, jump off a rock, fall in a hole. She picked up some big stones and threw them, hard.

The young man turned and ran, trying not to get hit by the stones. As he jumped on his horse, he shouted back angrily, 'Alright, you wait. I gunna report you to the police.'

Molly, woken by the noise, came running.

'What's wrong?' she called. 'Who are you screaming at?'

Daisy told her, and they watched the man riding away.

'Mongrel bastard,' Molly whispered angrily. 'Come on, we gotta move along, quickly.' They took the dead birds with them and walked until nightfall, when the shadows were long and they felt it was safe to make a fire to cook the birds.
꘡꘡/꘡꘡/꘡꘡/

The girls were now in their own land and knew every rock, every tree, every dry river bed. They walked long hours every day and, after meeting the cattle worker, they kept watch for strangers. They did not want to get caught so close to home.

News travels easily among desert people. At Jigalong the families knew about the escape and the long walk north, and knew the girls were getting close. Molly's mother, Maude, and old Granny Frinda spent many hours looking south, watching and waiting, and Maude used to whisper quietly,

'They're coming home. Our girls are coming home to us.'

Near Station 594 on the old cattle route Molly and Daisy knew there was a camp where one of their aunties lived. They had no food or water left, so when night came, they went on walking in the moonlight until they reached the camp.

Their aunty cried and cried when she saw them. 'You girls are so thin!' she said. She cooked them a meal, but they could eat very little because their stomachs were now so small.

'Your cousin Joey is going north tomorrow with some workers on the fence,' she said. 'You can go with him.'

Jigalong was still four days away, but it was not hard travelling, because Joey let them ride on a camel, and at night they had food and water and a safe place to sleep by the camp fire.

'They're coming home. Our girls are coming home to us.'

They passed Lake Nabberu, and came to Mundiwindi. Soon in the distance they could see the black hills where their families hunted for girdi-girdis and goannas.

On the fourth day they came to Jigalong. Molly and Daisy left Joey and began walking to their family camp. The end of their long, long journey had finally arrived, and they could feel their mothers waiting for them. In the clear evening light they ran across the dusty red earth of their homeland, and soon they disappeared into the trees round the camp. The Mardu daughters and granddaughters had come home.

By daybreak the next morning, the camp was empty. The families had disappeared into the Western Desert, taking their daughters and their granddaughters to places where the white man could not find them.

To Mr A. O. Neville

Chief Protector of Aborigines, Perth

The half-caste girls Molly and Daisy have returned to the Jigalong area after their most wonderful walk home. I am afraid you will never get them now. By this time they will be somewhere back in their own country, out in the desert – nobody knows where. I do not think you will ever keep them in a settlement unless you lock them up all the time. And I guess it is better for them to live in the bush than behind a locked door.

Arthur T. Hungerford

Superintendent, Jigalong Depot

11th October 1931

++++++++

Gracie was caught at Wiluna. When she arrived, her mother was not there, but Gracie decided to wait until she came to fetch her. She stayed with some Mardu people called Ned and Rosie in their camp. She told everybody her name was Lucy, but they still caught her, and sent her back to Moore River.

SEVENTY YEARS LATER

GRACIE

When Gracie was caught at Wiluna, she was kept there for some weeks and then finally sent back to Moore River Native Settlement. She went to school there and when she finished school, she was sent to work as a domestic servant on farms north of Perth, and on cattle stations up north of Geraldton. While she was working on a cattle station near Shark Bay on the coast, she met and married a young station worker named Harry Cross. They had six children: Lucina, Therese, Margaret, Marcia, Celine, and Clarence. After some years Gracie and her husband left each other, and Gracie moved to Geraldton. She died in 1983. Gracie never returned to Jigalong.

DAISY

After her return, Daisy moved with her family to a camp near Lake Nabberu, along the rabbit-proof fence south of Jigalong. She worked as a domestic servant on stations in the area. She married Kadibil, a station worker, and had four children: Noreena, Elizabeth, Jenny, and Margaret. After her husband's death, Daisy moved to Kalundi Seventh Day Adventist Mission, twenty-five kilometres north of Meekatharra, where she worked as a cook-housekeeper until the Mission closed in the 1970s. Daisy is a wonderful story-teller. She remembers those weeks back in 1931 so clearly, and it is because of her stories about that journey that this book was written. Daisy now lives with her daughters' families at Jigalong.

MOLLY

Molly worked as a domestic servant on Balfour Downs Station, north of Jigalong, where she married Toby Kelly. She had two daughters, Doris (the author of this story) and Annabelle. In November 1940 Molly became ill and had to go to hospital in Perth for a few weeks. When she came out, the government sent her back to Moore River Settlement with her two daughters. Nine months later, Molly had a letter from home, telling her of the deaths of some people in her family. She

The real Molly and Daisy, aged about 84 and 78 years, at Jigalong.

asked if she could go home to see her family, and the government refused to let her go.

In January 1941 Molly ran away from Moore River for the second time, taking eighteen-month-old Annabelle with her and leaving Doris (aged four years) behind at the settlement. She and her baby daughter arrived safely at Jigalong months later, following the same route that she had taken ten years earlier. She moved back to Balfour Downs with her husband Toby and baby Annabelle. Three years later Annabelle was taken away from Molly and sent to a children's home in the south. Molly has not seen her since.

Molly and Toby worked on stations around Meekatharra until they stopped working in 1972. Toby died in 1973. Molly now lives quietly at Jigalong, but she plays a big part in the Mardu community. In the big Aboriginal family Molly has eighteen grandchildren, twenty-nine great-grandchildren, and two great-great-grandchildren.

GLOSSARY

Aborigine a member of the people who were the original people of Australia; *adj* **Aboriginal**

acacia a kind of tree or bush that grows in dry places

bar a long straight piece of metal or wood

bastard *(taboo, slang)* a rude word for a man who has been unpleasant or cruel

billycan *(Australian English)* a metal can used for boiling water

bucket an open container used for carrying liquids

bush *(Australian English)* wild land that has not been cleared

bush a plant that grows like a short, thick tree

camp *(n & v)* a place where people live for a short time

cattle cows and bulls that are kept as farm animals

constable a junior police officer

crouch *(v)* to put your body close to the ground by bending your legs under you

damper *(Australian English)* flat bread

depot a place where food, vehicles, and other things are kept

desert *(n)* a large area of land that has very little water and very few plants growing on it

direction where a person or thing is going or looking

distance the amount of space between two places or things

domestic servant somebody who works in another person's house, doing the cleaning and other jobs

dormitory a room for several people to sleep in

fence a thing like a wall made of pieces of wood joined by wires

flour a white powder used in cooking for making bread

footprint a mark left on the ground by a person's foot or shoe

goanna *(Australian English)* a lizard

gotta *(Australian spoken English)* got to

government the group of people who control a country

grief great sadness, often because somebody has died

gunna *(Australian spoken English)* going to

half-caste *(offensive, not used today)* a person whose parents are from different races; today, we say 'a person **of mixed race**'

hunt *(v)* to chase wild animals or birds in order to catch or kill them for food

kangaroo an Australian animal that jumps on its strong back legs

landmark something (a building, a hill, a tree, a fence, etc.) that you can see clearly and that helps you to know where you are

law a rule of a country that says what people may or may not do

lizard a small animal that has four short legs, a long tail, and a rough skin

mongrel a dog that is a mixture of different breeds

nest a place where a bird keeps its eggs or its babies

protector somebody who makes sure that other people are kept safe, and not harmed or used badly

rabbit a small animal with long ears

safety being safe; not in danger

scared frightened

settlement a place where people have come to live

shelter *(n)* a place that protects you from weather or danger

sore *(n & adj)* a painful place on your body

spine on a plant, a sharp pointed part like a needle

store *(n)* a shop

superintendent an important government official

tears water that comes from the eyes

telegram a message sent by telephone and then printed and given to someone

track *(v)* to follow someone by the marks that they have left
    behind them on the ground; **tracker** *(n)* a person who does this
track *(n)* marks left by a person or animal; also, a rough path
tucker *(Australian English)* food
verandah a platform with an open front and a roof, built onto
    the side of a house
well *(n)* a deep hole in the ground from which people can get
    water
white man an expression meaning all white men, all Europeans
    with pale skin

MARDU WORDS USED IN THE STORY

dgudu older sister   **muda-muda** half-caste
girdi-girdi a hill kangaroo   **wudgebulla** white man

Before Reading

1 Read the story introduction on the first page of the book, and the back cover. How much do you know now about the story? Choose T (True) or F (False) for each sentence.

1 Molly, Daisy, and Gracie were the children of Aboriginal fathers and white mothers. T / F

2 Molly was the oldest of the three children. T / F

3 The Aborigines came to Australia from Europe. T / F

4 The Australian government took half-caste children away from their families and sent them to settlements. T / F

5 The government wanted half-caste children to behave and live like white people. T / F

6 The three girls escaped and went home by train. T / F

7 They followed the rabbit-proof fence to get home. T / F

8 The story is told by Daisy's son. T / F

2 Can you guess which of these things happens in the story? Choose as many as you like.

1 The girls hunt animals and kill them for food.

2 People that they meet give them food.

3 They hide in the day and travel only at night.

4 One of them gets very ill and nearly dies.

5 The three girls stay together right till the end.

6 The police chase them but never catch up with them.

ACTIVITIES

While Reading

Read *The Fence* and Chapters 1 and 2, and answer these questions.

1 Why did the government build the fence?
2 Why were orders given about Molly, Gracie, and Daisy?
3 How did the three girls travel to Moore River Settlement?
4 How did they feel when they got there?

Before you read Chapter 3, can you guess what happens? Choose one answer for each question.

1 Which of the three girls decides they must escape?
   a) Molly   b) Gracie   c) Daisy
2 How soon after arriving does she decide to escape?
   a) the next day   b) a week later   c) three weeks later
3 How do the other two girls feel about escaping?
   a) happy   b) excited   c) scared

Read Chapters 3 and 4, and answer these questions.

Who . . .?
1 . . . were beaten and had all their hair cut off?
2 . . . always went after any runaways and caught them?
3 . . . had the idea of sleeping in a rabbit hole?
4 . . . gave the girls a cooked kangaroo tail?
5 . . . went to the farmhouse to ask for something to eat?

Before you read Chapter 5, try to guess what happens. Choose as many of these ideas as you like.

The woman at the farmhouse . . .

1 shouts at them and tells them to go away.
2 gives them food and some warm coats.
3 phones the superintendent at the Moore River Settlement.

Read Chapters 5 and 6, and complete these sentences in your own words.

1 Sometimes Molly carried the other two girls, because . . .
2 When they found the fence, they did not know that . . .
3 Don Willocks gave the girls food, but later he . . .
4 The girls never walked close to the fence because they . . .

Before you read Chapter 7 (*Losing Gracie*), what do you think is going to happen? Choose one of these ideas.

1 Gracie gets very ill and has to go to hospital.
2 The police chase Gracie and catch her.
3 Gracie decides to leave the other two and catch a train.
4 Gracie disappears in the night and is never seen again.

Read Chapter 7 and *Seventy Years Later*, and complete these sentences with the right names.

1 _____ never returned to Jigalong.
2 Ten years later _____ was sent back to Moore River.
3 _____'s daughter Doris was left behind at Moore River.
4 _____ and _____ lived at Jigalong as old ladies.

ACTIVITIES

After Reading

1 Complete these two newspaper reports about the Jigalong girls, using the words below (one word for each gap). The two headlines also need one word from the list.

best, better, chance, cooking, escaped, failed, families, fire, home, hunted, law, money, rabbits, scared, school, shelters, spend, tracks, ungrateful, useful, walking, weeks, wonderful

1
_____ ABORIGINAL GIRLS

The government has _____ to catch the half-caste girls who _____ from Moore River Settlement several _____ ago. A lot of _____ has been spent on these children, but if they do not want the _____ to make a _____ life for themselves, why make them go to _____? We should _____ the money on more _____ things, and the _____ about these Aboriginal children must be changed.

2
_____ ABORIGINAL GIRLS

They were cold, hungry, and _____ most of the time, but they never stopped _____. They _____ for their food, catching _____, lizards, and birds, and _____ them over a fire. They built _____ every night, pulled them down in the mornings, covered their _____ holes, and were careful not to leave easy _____ for the police to follow. They just wanted to get _____ to their _____, and that's the _____ place for any child to be.

63

2 Here are Martha and Polly talking in the evening of the day when the three Jigalong girls ran away. Write in the names for each speaker, and put their conversation in the right order. Martha speaks first, at number 3.

1 _____ 'Yes, he has. But he's not going to catch these three. I've got a feeling about it.'

2 _____ 'Oh yeah, of course! That Molly's a clever one, for sure. Do you think they'll get all the way home?'

3 _____ 'Heard the news?'

4 _____ 'Well, yes, but what difference does the rain make?'

5 _____ 'This morning. They never came to school at all, but nobody realized that till this evening.'

6 _____ 'No, what is it? Tell me!'

7 _____ 'Don't know. Jigalong's a long, long way. But I hope they do.'

8 _____ 'So that means they've had all day. Has Moodoo gone after them?'

9 _____ 'I'll tell you why not. Because it rained most of the afternoon, didn't it?'

10 _____ 'Escaped! They only arrived two days ago. When did they go?'

11 _____ 'Moodoo's a tracker, right? But he can't follow tracks if the rain has washed them all away!'

12 _____ 'So do I. Good luck to them, I say!'

13 _____ 'Those three new girls from Jigalong. Molly, and the younger two. They've gone – escaped!'

14 _____ 'Why not? He's always caught the other runaways.'

3 There are 12 words (they are all 5 letters or longer) hidden in this word search. Find the words, and draw lines through them. Words go from left to right, and from top to bottom.

```
T  H  G  E  G  I  L  R  F  L  T  S  N  E
A  B  O  R  I  G  I  N  E  E  R  D  F  A
B  E  V  T  R  T  Z  E  N  R  A  C  O  H
A  N  E  C  A  E  A  I  C  N  C  R  O  L
I  F  R  E  B  T  R  H  E  A  K  U  T  N
T  H  N  E  B  Y  D  C  A  N  G  N  P  E
T  O  M  U  I  T  L  A  N  D  M  A  R  K
S  H  E  L  T  E  R  H  E  R  E  W  I  I
K  A  N  G  A  R  O  O  N  T  H  A  N  E
B  U  T  S  P  A  D  L  O  C  K  Y  T  H
```

Now put the 12 words into 3 groups, under these headings:

PEOPLE   ANIMALS   THINGS

4 Now write down all the letters in the word search that don't have a line through them. Begin with the first line, and go across each line to the end. You should have 61 letters, which will make a sentence of 17 words. What is the sentence?

1 Who said or wrote this sentence in the story?
2 Who was he or she speaking or writing about?
3 What did he or she mean by these words?
4 Do you agree with this sentence? Why or why not?
5 The words were said or written more than seventy years ago. Do you think things have changed since then?

5 **What did you think about some of the people in this story? Make some sentences with these names and adjectives.**

Constable Riggs / Mrs Flanagan / Mr Hungerford / Don Willocks

1 _____ was *right / wrong* to _____
2 _____ was *kind / unkind* when _____

6 **You can read about the author of this story, Doris Pilkington Garimara, on pages 67 to 69. Read those pages, and then talk about these questions.**

1 What for you is the saddest thing in the story of Molly and her two daughters, Doris and Annabelle?
2 What for you is the happiest thing in their story?

7 **The Aborigines were the first people in Australia; the Europeans arrived later. Did new people ever come to your country in the past? There are often difficulties when that happens. Think of some advice to complete these sentences.**

1 People coming to a new country must _____
2 People coming to a new country must not _____
3 People coming to a new country should _____
4 People coming to a new country should not _____
5 People coming to a new country should try to _____
6 People coming to a new country should try not to

_____

ABOUT THE AUTHOR,
THE BOOK, AND THE FILM

Doris Pilkington Garimara was born on Balfour Downs Station about sixty kilometres northwest of Jigalong in the East Pilbara district. In 1940, aged about four years old, Doris and her mother Molly and her baby sister Annabelle were forcibly brought from Jigalong to Moore River Native Settlement. Months later, Molly escaped and walked back to Jigalong, carrying the baby Annabelle, but leaving Doris behind as she could not carry both children.

When she was twelve, Doris was taken to the Roelands Mission, where the missionaries, she wrote, 'brought her up to believe Aboriginal people were dirty and evil'. She finished school and left Roelands, the first from the mission to begin nursing training at the Royal Perth Hospital. Her married life was spent in Geraldton with her husband and six children. She returned to Perth to continue her studies at university, and later studied journalism. Then she worked in film/video production with the Western Australian Institute of Film and Television.

For a long time Doris Pilkington was angry about the past. But before she left Moore River, an aunt had told her: 'Don't forget who you are. Your mother's name is Molly Craig and you come from Balfour Downs.' And at Christmas 1962, when she was twenty-five, Doris found her parents again.

'I took the journey back to my land at Jigalong in Western Australia,' she wrote. 'I took my children to walk on my hot, dusty land. It was then that I was reunited with my mother.' She also got to know the father she had never really known, and many other relatives, but it was not until 1986 that she heard from her aunt Daisy the story of her mother's first escape from Moore River in 1931. 'Aunt Daisy told me her memories,' Doris said, 'and as soon as she finished talking, I wrote it down and vowed to fill in the missing pieces later on.'

Doris kept this promise to record her family's history. In 1990 her manuscript entry, *Caprice: A Stockman's Daughter*, won the David Unaipon Award for unpublished Aboriginal and Torres Strait Islander writers, and was published in 1991. *Follow the Rabbit-Proof Fence* was published in 1996, and in 2002 was produced as the film *Rabbit-Proof Fence*, directed by Phillip Noyce. She wrote a third book, *Under the Windamarra Tree*, which was published in 2003 and completes her *Nungar* trilogy, the story of the women of her family over three generations. 'In the life of an Aboriginal woman,' Doris writes, 'no one is more important than her mother when she is young, her daughters when she is old.'

When making the film of *Rabbit-Proof Fence*, the Australian director Phillip Noyce chose completely untrained Aboriginal children to play the parts of Molly, Gracie, and Daisy. They gave astonishing performances, and the film quickly became a success all around the world. It won a great number of prizes, created quite a political storm in Australia, and made many people think hard about how aboriginal people everywhere are treated by their governments.

The best moment for Doris was when the film was shown at Jigalong in January 2002. It was in the open air in the school playground, in front of several hundred people. As the film began, the sun was setting and the sky over the Western Desert was brilliant with red, orange, and purple clouds. 'It was the first time that many Aborigines there had seen a film on a big screen,' she said. 'It was a very exciting moment. Even the men were crying and coming up to give me a hug.'

Since then she has travelled with Phillip Noyce all over the world to promote the film, talking about her own experiences, and hearing local stories of the suffering of native peoples.

'Back home,' she said, 'my mother and Daisy became famous. So many people have seen the film, then decided to go to Jigalong and visit them that the area has become a tourist attraction. Everyone is proud of those two old ladies. Everyone knows about the rabbit-proof fence. And everyone knows that they walked a long, long way.'

Molly Kelly died at Jigalong in January 2004, never having seen her daughter Annabelle again. Annabelle had been taken away from Molly at the age of three. Like so many other children, she had been taught to believe she was an orphan, and in later life chose not to recognize her Aboriginal past.

The laws that separated Molly from her mother, and later from her children, were finally changed in the 1960s. A famous report about the laws, called *Bringing Them Home*, was published in 1997. This revealed in many personal stories the long-term misery and suffering of thousands of Aboriginal families, the 'Stolen Generations' torn apart by the government's laws.

'I have reclaimed my history, my culture, my family,' Doris Pilkington has said. 'But there are people all over Australia who have seen the film and who are now, for the first time, talking about their history and their experiences. It's a painful time for them. But many Aboriginal women have said to me, "Now I'm going to search for my family. I want to go home".'

OXFORD BOOKWORMS LIBRARY

Classics • Crime & Mystery • Factfiles • Fantasy & Horror
Human Interest • Playscripts • Thriller & Adventure
True Stories • World Stories

The OXFORD BOOKWORMS LIBRARY provides enjoyable reading in English, with a wide range of classic and modern fiction, non-fiction, and plays. It includes original and adapted texts in seven carefully graded language stages, which take learners from beginner to advanced level. An overview is given on the next pages.

All Stage 1 titles are available as audio recordings, as well as over eighty other titles from Starter to Stage 6. All Starters and many titles at Stages 1 to 4 are specially recommended for younger learners. Every Bookworm is illustrated, and Starters and Factfiles have full-colour illustrations.

The OXFORD BOOKWORMS LIBRARY also offers extensive support. Each book contains an introduction to the story, notes about the author, a glossary, and activities. Additional resources include tests and worksheets, and answers for these and for the activities in the books. There is advice on running a class library, using audio recordings, and the many ways of using Oxford Bookworms in reading programmes. Resource materials are available on the website <www.oup.com/bookworms>.

The *Oxford Bookworms Collection* is a series for advanced learners. It consists of volumes of short stories by well-known authors, both classic and modern. Texts are not abridged or adapted in any way, but carefully selected to be accessible to the advanced student.

You can find details and a full list of titles in the *Oxford Bookworms Library Catalogue* and *Oxford English Language Teaching Catalogues*, and on the website <www.oup.com/bookworms>.

THE OXFORD BOOKWORMS LIBRARY
GRADING AND SAMPLE EXTRACTS

STARTER • 250 HEADWORDS

present simple – present continuous – imperative –
can/cannot, must – *going to* (future) – simple gerunds …

Her phone is ringing – but where is it?

Sally gets out of bed and looks in her bag. No phone. She looks under the bed. No phone. Then she looks behind the door. There is her phone. Sally picks up her phone and answers it. *Sally's Phone*

STAGE 1 • 400 HEADWORDS

… past simple – coordination with *and, but, or* –
subordination with *before, after, when, because, so* …

I knew him in Persia. He was a famous builder and I worked with him there. For a time I was his friend, but not for long. When he came to Paris, I came after him – I wanted to watch him. He was a very clever, very dangerous man. *The Phantom of the Opera*

STAGE 2 • 700 HEADWORDS

… present perfect – *will* (future) – *(don't) have to, must not, could* –
comparison of adjectives – simple *if* clauses – past continuous –
tag questions – *ask/tell* + infinitive …

While I was writing these words in my diary, I decided what to do. I must try to escape. I shall try to get down the wall outside. The window is high above the ground, but I have to try. I shall take some of the gold with me – if I escape, perhaps it will be helpful later. *Dracula*

... *should, may* – present perfect continuous – *used to* – past perfect –
causative – relative clauses – indirect statements ...

Of course, it was most important that no one should see
Colin, Mary, or Dickon entering the secret garden. So Colin
gave orders to the gardeners that they must all keep away
from that part of the garden in future. *The Secret Garden*

STAGE 4 • 1400 HEADWORDS

... past perfect continuous – passive (simple forms) –
would conditional clauses – indirect questions –
relatives with *where/when* – gerunds after prepositions/phrases ...

I was glad. Now Hyde could not show his face to the world
again. If he did, every honest man in London would be proud
to report him to the police. *Dr Jekyll and Mr Hyde*

STAGE 5 • 1800 HEADWORDS

... future continuous – future perfect –
passive (modals, continuous forms) –
would have conditional clauses – modals + perfect infinitive ...

If he had spoken Estella's name, I would have hit him. I was so
angry with him, and so depressed about my future, that I could
not eat the breakfast. Instead I went straight to the old house.
Great Expectations

STAGE 6 • 2500 HEADWORDS

... passive (infinitives, gerunds) – advanced modal meanings –
clauses of concession, condition

When I stepped up to the piano, I was confident. It was as if I
knew that the prodigy side of me really did exist. And when I
started to play, I was so caught up in how lovely I looked that
I didn't worry how I would sound. *The Joy Luck Club*